Original title:
Starry Chill

Copyright © 2024 Swan Charm
All rights reserved.

Author: Daisy Dewi
ISBN HARDBACK: 978-9908-52-035-3
ISBN PAPERBACK: 978-9908-52-036-0
ISBN EBOOK: 978-9908-52-037-7

Hushed Whispers of Ethereal Chill

In twilight's grasp, the shadows play,
Soft murmurs dance in fading light.
The air, a canvas, cool and gray,
As stars awaken, bold and bright.

Beneath the trees where silence swells,
The rustle sings of secrets old.
A gentle breeze its story tells,
In whispered tones, both calm and bold.

Moonlight weaves through branches thin,
Caressing earth with silver thread.
In nature's arms, where dreams begin,
The echo of the night is fed.

The chill wraps round, a soft embrace,
Holding thoughts like autumn leaves.
In every corner, time will trace,
The magic that the stillness weaves.

So listen close to these sweet sighs,
The hush invites the heart to still.
In every pause, the spirit flies,
To find the peace of twilight's thrill.

Veil of the Heavens

Stars twinkle softly, a distant embrace,
Whispers of night dance, a timeless grace.
Beneath the vast sky, dreams take their flight,
Wrapped in the silence, bathed in moonlight.

Clouds drift like shadows, secrets to share,
Echoes of starlight linger in the air.
Moments of calm in the night's gentle sigh,
Veils of the heavens, where wishes may lie.

A Glint of Dream

In the quiet corners, a soft light shines,
Flickers of hope in the heart's fragile lines.
A glint of a dream, both fleeting and rare,
Guiding the soul through the depths of despair.

Eyes closed in wonder, a journey begins,
Woven in shadows, where silence wins.
Fragments of laughter, lost in the seam,
Forever held close, this glint of a dream.

Moonlit Frost

Under the pale glow, the world is aglow,
Frost kisses petals, their beauty made slow.
Crystals are sprinkled, a soft, silver touch,
Whispers of winter, it paints oh so much.

The silence is golden, the stillness immense,
Moments of wonder, a delicate tense.
Softly the night falls, as time holds its breath,
Moonlit frost glistens, a dance with sweet death.

Radiance in the Cold

Amidst biting winds, a light starts to beam,
A warmth that arises, igniting a dream.
Radiance echoes through crystals of ice,
Bringing forth beauty amid the device.

In the frosty air, embers start to glow,
Guiding lost wanderers, their way through the snow.
Each flicker a promise, a heart brave and bold,
Revealing the magic, a radiance in the cold.

Selene's Touch

In the quiet night so pale,
Selene whispers with her veil,
Casting light on dreams anew,
Softly guiding hearts so true.

Moonbeams dance on silver streams,
Mending shadows, weaving dreams,
A gentle touch, a tender sigh,
In her glow, our spirits fly.

Stars align, a cosmic kiss,
In her presence, we find bliss,
Each reflection ripples wide,
Underneath the celestial tide.

Through the trees, her secrets roam,
Illuminating paths back home,
In the silence, we all find,
The magic woven through the kind.

A lullaby of nightly grace,
In her arms, the world finds space,
Breath of night, a promise made,
In her light, all fears do fade.

Chilling Radiance

The night descends with icy breath,
A chilling glow, the whispers of death,
Crystals form in the air so still,
Under the moon, they bend to will.

Glistening frost on every tree,
A shimm'ring dance, wild and free,
Chilling radiance, sharp and bright,
A spectral glow in the heart of night.

Beneath the stars, the shadows play,
In the cold, the warmth gives way,
A canvas painted in hues of blue,
Where silence speaks, and dreams break through.

Echoes of the past resound,
In this silence, secrets found,
The air is thick with stories lost,
In chilling radiance, we pay the cost.

Fragments scatter, they drift away,
Embrace the night, let darkness sway,
In every shadow, a flicker of light,
A chilling dawn waits for the night.

Resonance of the Night

In the stillness, whispers rise,
The resonance of hidden ties,
A song of moonlight on the breeze,
Rustling leaves, ancient trees.

Echoes dance through the empty street,
Nighttime's pulse, a rhythmic beat,
Stars aligned, a cosmic lure,
Searching hearts feel the allure.

Between the shadows, secrets hum,
Drawing forth the dreams that come,
In the darkness, stories weave,
From the echoes, we believe.

Each heartbeat thrums a soft refrain,
In the night, we find our gain,
Resonance flows like water's grace,
In the still, we find our place.

Guided by the night's embrace,
Every moment we must chase,
In this silence, time stands still,
With each breath, we feel the thrill.

Symphony of the Stars

Under velvet skies, they shine,
Each star a note, a sacred line,
A symphony that lights the night,
Creating beauty, pure delight.

Twinkling notes in cosmic dance,
Guiding souls with every glance,
In the stillness, melodies play,
Whispers of the night's ballet.

Celestial winds carry the song,
Where dreams and stardust both belong,
In harmony, the worlds unite,
A symphony that feels so right.

Echoed laughter from afar,
In this chorus, we reach for stars,
Each moment, a fleeting chord,
In the silence, we find reward.

As the night unfolds its grace,
Every heartbeat finds its place,
In the beauty of the darkened skies,
Symphony of stars, where magic lies.

Whispering Stars in a Frosted Landscape

In the stillness of the night,
Whispers dance on frozen air.
Stars twinkle with gentle light,
Secrets held in their bright glare.

Snowflakes fall like softest dreams,
Blanketing the world in white.
Nature's magic softly beams,
A tapestry of pure delight.

Beneath the moon's soft embrace,
Shadows weave in quiet grace.
Each breath lingers in the cold,
Tales of wonder to unfold.

The trees wear silver crowns of frost,
Silent guardians of the night.
Every moment feels embossed,
In the glow of pale moonlight.

Hearts are warmed by starlit glow,
In this realm where magic sings.
Whispering secrets soft and slow,
In the frost, the night takes wings.

The Chill of Cosmic Reflections

In the mirror of the sea,
Stars shine bright like silver coins.
Echoes drift both wild and free,
A cosmic song that still enjoins.

Chill descends on silent night,
Ripples catch the starlit gleam.
Each reflection holds the light,
Of dreams born from a midnight dream.

The vastness calls without a sound,
A stillness deep and sincere.
In its arms, lost souls are found,
Casting off all earthly fear.

Frozen realms beneath the dark,
Ice reflects a thousand skies.
In this beauty, we embark,
To seek the truth beneath the lies.

Through the chill we find our way,
Guided by the cosmic stream.
In the night, where shadows play,
We awaken from our dream.

Starlit Frost on Silent Waters

Moonlit ripples softly play,
Frost collects on liquid dreams.
Stars reflect in quiet sway,
Nature's hush in silver beams.

Each wave carries whispered sound,
Calm and peace reside within.
In this world, no pain is found,
Just the night and stars that spin.

The chill wraps around like lace,
Embracing calm in every breath.
Bright reflections leave no trace,
A beauty fierce, untouched by death.

Silent waters hold the night,
Cradling dreams in still embrace.
Glowing softly, pure and bright,
Time unmoving, a sacred space.

In this realm where starlight dwells,
Whispers drift on tranquil tides.
Every secret softly tells,
Of the peace that silence hides.

Elysian Ice Beneath the Astral Vault

A vast expanse of frozen peace,
Where stars weave tales across the night.
Breath of winter brings release,
A canvas painted pure and white.

Underneath the astral dome,
Whispers weave through crystal air.
In this realm, we find a home,
Where the heart feels light as air.

Icy breath on barest skin,
Tingles spark like fireworks bright.
Elysian moments, deep within,
In unity with the night.

The frost lays down a gentle kiss,
On every surface, every stone.
In this beauty, we find bliss,
The starry sky, we're not alone.

Here we dance with shadows cast,
United by the chilly grace.
Elysium found at last,
In the stars' warm, cold embrace.

Awakening the Night

The moon whispers soft and bright,
Stars shimmer in velvet night,
Shadows dance on ancient trees,
Awakening whispers carried by the breeze.

Night creatures stir from their sleep,
Secrets in darkness, promises they keep,
A symphony of whispers fills the air,
Awakening mysteries, dreams laid bare.

The cool ground beneath their feet,
Crickets sing, all sounds discreet,
With every rustle, a heart ignites,
Awakening embers of soft delights.

Through moonlit paths, we tread anew,
In the depth of night, a journey too,
Hand in hand, our spirits soar,
Awakening together, forevermore.

Dreams Under a Veil

Beneath a veil, we weave our fate,
In dreams where love and hope await,
Silent wishes on gentle sighs,
An ethereal dance beneath the skies.

Whispers float like mist at dawn,
In shadowed realms where fears are gone,
Colorful visions, tender embrace,
Dreams under a veil, a sacred space.

Each heartbeat pulls the fabric tight,
Stitched with stars, painted in light,
A tapestry of longing and grace,
Dreams under a veil, our secret place.

In this stillness, we find our song,
Where day and night forever belong,
With every breath, our spirits rise,
Dreams under a veil, where love never dies.

Crystal Echoes

In caverns deep, where silence sings,
Crystal echoes of ancient things,
Flickering lights on jagged stone,
Whispers of the past, we call our own.

Each drop of water, a song of time,
Reflections shimmer, shadows climb,
The heartbeat of earth, in rhythm flows,
Crystal echoes, where wisdom grows.

Through the stillness, we hear their song,
Vocal gems that last so long,
Nature's chorus, a gentle plea,
Crystal echoes, setting spirits free.

In every glimmer, a story told,
Of fire and ice, both brave and bold,
Guiding our steps, lighting the way,
Crystal echoes, come what may.

Nebula's Embrace

In the cosmos, where colors blend,
Nebula's embrace, a cosmic friend,
Stars are born in tender light,
A cradle of dreams, vast and bright.

Galaxies swirl in a dance so grand,
Embracing the night, hand in hand,
Celestial bodies, a painter's brush,
Nebula's embrace, in silence, hush.

Each twinkling gem, a wish anew,
Stories crafted from stardust, too,
In this vastness, we find our place,
Nebula's embrace, a warm embrace.

Floating softly through cosmic streams,
Life unfolds in nebula dreams,
Eternal, boundless, forever we roam,
Nebula's embrace, our celestial home.

Glimmering Silence

In the stillness of the night,
Stars whisper softly bright.
Voices linger in the air,
Secrets held without a care.

Moonlight dances on the ground,
Painting shadows all around.
Night's embrace, a gentle sigh,
Time has ceased to pass us by.

Hidden dreams begin to bloom,
Filling up the quiet room.
Every heartbeat feels so loud,
Wrapped within this velvet shroud.

Glimmering echoes start to fade,
In the silence, thoughts cascade.
Fleeting moments drift apart,
Tugging softly at the heart.

As dawn's breath begins to rise,
Colors paint the waking skies.
Yet in daylight's bright embrace,
Whispers linger in their place.

Breath of the Night

Underneath the shrouded sky,
Crickets sing a lullaby.
Gentle winds, a soft caress,
Bringing forth a sweet recess.

Shadows stretch beneath the trees,
Carried by the evening breeze.
Stars awaken one by one,
Chasing dreams until they're done.

The moon, a watchful guiding light,
Illuminates the heart's delight.
Each moment in this tranquil space,
A fleeting breath, a warm embrace.

In these hours, time stands still,
Nature's hush becomes a thrill.
Every sigh, a sacred tone,
In the night, we're not alone.

As dawn begins to hold its sway,
Shadows fade and dreams decay.
Yet the breath of night remains,
In whispered echoes and refrains.

Veiled in Frost

Morning breaks with silver sheen,
Nature wears her frost-filled queen.
Each blade glimmers, crystal made,
Hidden worlds in cold displayed.

Branches whisper, softly creak,
In frozen silence, trees unique.
Air is brisk with winter's breath,
A gentle muse that speaks of death.

Footsteps crunch on icy ground,
Joy in stillness can be found.
Promises of spring may tease,
Yet now, winter's heart does freeze.

Clouds above, a muted gray,
Veiled in frost, the world at bay.
Nature pauses, takes a breath,
In this moment, life and death.

As shadows lengthen, daylight wanes,
Silent beauty still remains.
Veiled in frost, we find our peace,
In winter's grip, our hearts release.

Luminous Cold

Underneath a midnight glow,
Snowflakes dance and softly flow.
A world transformed in tranquil white,
Whispers fill the starry night.

Breath of winter, crisp and clear,
Silent echoes, drawing near.
Each twinkle sparkles, crisp and bold,
In the heart, a story told.

Frozen lakes, reflections bright,
Mirror worlds in pale moonlight.
Time stands still, the air is pure,
In this quiet, we find sure.

Luminous visions come to play,
Dreams unfold in silver sway.
Every moment, frozen glow,
Lifts the spirit, soft and slow.

As the dawn begins to creep,
Colors in the silence seep.
In luminous cold, we find our way,
Blessed by night before the day.

The Night's Enigmatic Chill

In shadows deep, where whispers creep,
The moonlight bathes the silent steep.
Chill dances through the breath of trees,
A symphony on midnight's breeze.

Stars ignite in the velvet sky,
Secrets held where dreams lie shy.
Each twinkle a tale, a silent plea,
To uncover the night's mystery.

Frosted whispers caress the air,
A haunting song, both sweet and rare.
The clock ticks softly, time stands still,
Wrapped in the night's enigmatic chill.

Echoes of dreams, both old and new,
Float like feathers, light and few.
Each sigh a shadow, softly spun,
Until the threads of dawn are begun.

The darkness fades as morning lights,
But echoes linger, soft as rights.
Though day may break, the night will stay,
In memories where darkness plays.

Whispered Legacies of the Night

In the stillness of the darkened hour,
Whispered legacies begin to flower.
Voices linger on the strands of air,
Carrying secrets beyond despair.

Tales of lovers lost to time,
Echo through the night's soft rhyme.
The pulse of hearts in twilight's grasp,
Hold onto dreams with a gentle clasp.

Stars like lanterns in a hidden maze,
Guide us through an ancient haze.
Each breath a promise, every sigh,
A memory of what cannot die.

Moonlit dances on the edge of fate,
Every shadow holds a regal state.
Yet in silence, the stories blend,
Whispered legacies that transcend.

As dawn approaches, softly glows,
The night unveils what time bestows.
In whispered tones, the night's embrace,
Echoes still in a timeless space.

Fractured Light in the Arctic Abyss

In the heart of cold, where whispers freeze,
Fractured light dances on the seas.
Icebergs shimmer, a crystal dream,
Reflecting chaos in the quiet stream.

The northern winds weave tales of old,
Stories of warmth in the freezing cold.
Each fracture a glimpse, a fleeting sight,
Of shadows trapped in ethereal light.

Beneath the surface, secrets lie,
Like ancient ruins lost to the sky.
The pulse of time in the icy deep,
Holds memories that we long to keep.

Snowflakes whisper their fragile fate,
Each one unique, delicate weight.
In the dark abyss, where echoes sigh,
Fractured light twinkles as dreams drift by.

With dawn approaching, a new day breaks,
Yet the whispers of night still gently wake.
In the depths below, the stories flow,
Fractured light in the Arctic's glow.

Celestial Frost on the Edge of Sleep

In the twilight haze where dreams conspire,
Celestial frost ignites the fire.
Softly it settles on eyelids drawn,
Whispering tales till the break of dawn.

Stars twinkle bright in the velvet night,
Guiding the heart with gentle light.
Each breath a shimmer, laced with grace,
Time suspends in this sacred space.

Silent whispers of the cosmic sea,
Wrap us close with a tender plea.
Floating softly on the edge of sleep,
In a world where secrets softly seep.

Cold kisses linger upon the skin,
Drawing us deeper where dreams begin.
The universe hums a lullaby song,
In the celestial dance where we belong.

Morning aches to break the spell,
Yet in our hearts, the echoes dwell.
For within the frost, our dreams take flight,
Celestial wonders born from the night.

Frozen Galaxies

In the depths of a frozen space,
Time drifts in a spectral race,
Stars like diamonds quietly gleam,
Encased in an icy dream.

Nebulas whisper tales untold,
Of cosmic wonders and stars of old,
A universe trapped in bluing light,
Capturing hearts in the night.

Planets spin in a frozen ballet,
Dancing in silence, they sway and play,
Each one a story, a spark of fate,
In the great cosmic state.

Light years pass, yet they remain,
Guardians of the cold terrain,
Frosted realms where shadows blend,
In the dark, where dreams ascend.

Embered cores in a chilling sea,
Frozen galaxies call to me,
Through the void, I hear their song,
In the silence, I long to belong.

Starlit Shadows

Under the veil of twilight skies,
Starlit shadows weave and rise,
Whispers of dreams on gentle air,
Filling the night with a tender glare.

Echoing soft in the cool dark night,
Every twinkle a moment of light,
Fleeting glimpses of what might be,
Caught in the dance of eternity.

Creatures of dusk begin to stir,
Kissed by twilight, they softly purr,
Nature blooms in the moon's caress,
A tranquil world, a soft finesse.

Glimmers of hope, shadows will cast,
Fading memories of a day past,
Each star a tear, each night a sigh,
In starlit shadows, we laugh and cry.

In the embrace of celestial light,
Starlit shadows take to flight,
Bringing dreams that softly flow,
Guiding us where love will grow.

Nightfall's Embrace

As day surrenders to dusk's sweet call,
Nightfall's embrace blankets all,
Stars awaken, bright and bold,
Casting tales of love retold.

The moon rises with silver grace,
Glimmers of light in the quiet space,
Whispers of night softly sigh,
As shadows dance in the sky.

With every heartbeat, silence sings,
A lullaby of gentle springs,
Wrapped in the comfort of soft night,
Finding solace in the light.

Dreamers wander through starlit trails,
Floating free as the night prevails,
In the cradle of darkened skies,
Where aspirations learn to rise.

Nightfall, a canvas, vast and deep,
Holds secrets of hearts that we keep,
In shadows' embrace, we find our place,
In the stillness, love leaves a trace.

Ethereal Glimmers

In a world where spirits roam,
Ethereal glimmers feel like home,
Dancing lights in a spectral haze,
Whirling tales of lost days.

Beneath the veil of a twilight sky,
Softly they whisper, flutter, and fly,
Guiding dreams with a golden thread,
In the quiet night where hope is fed.

Every flicker tells a story,
Of fleeting moments and faded glory,
A symphony sung by the breeze,
In harmony with the ancient trees.

Glimmers of light break through the dark,
Illuminating paths, a guiding spark,
Where wishes linger, softly strewn,
Beneath the watchful, silver moon.

Ethereal glimmers, a fleeting sight,
Casting joy through the endless night,
In their glow, we find our peace,
As the stars in the heavens cease.

Winter's Midnight Waltz

Snowflakes dance in the silver light,
Branches bow in the quiet night.
Whispers glide on the chilled breeze,
Time stands still, the world at ease.

Softly falls a blanket white,
Moonbeams twinkle, oh what a sight!
Footsteps crunch on the frozen ground,
Winter's beauty is all around.

Frosted windows, warmth within,
Laughter echoes, where hearts begin.
Cocoa steaming, stories shared,
In this season, love is bared.

Stars above in silence glow,
As the soft winds begin to blow.
Nature's waltz in rhythmic flow,
Holding dreams in winter's show.

Fleeting moments of pure bliss,
Captured in a tender kiss.
In winter's arms, we lose our fears,
Together dancing through the years.

Celestial Whispers

In the stillness of the night,
Stars are scattered, pure delight.
Galaxies spin in cosmic grace,
Whispers drift through endless space.

Comets draw their shining trails,
Stories woven in silken veils.
The moon, a guardian up high,
Watches over, as time goes by.

Softly, the universe sings,
Of ancient dreams and hidden things.
A cosmic dance, a fleeting chance,
In starlit skies, our hearts will prance.

Nebulas bloom in vibrant hues,
Painting the night with cosmic views.
Celestial secrets softly found,
In this silence, peace abounds.

Between the breaths of night and dawn,
Echoes of eternity drawn.
In quietude, we feel the pull,
Of cosmic love, forever full.

Chilled Reverie

In the frost of morning's light,
Dreams weave through the chilly night.
Silken mists on quiet streams,
Guide our hopes and whispered dreams.

Shadows dance upon the lake,
Leaves that shimmer, hearts awake.
Nature's breath, a soft caress,
In this moment, we find rest.

Eyes closed tight against the cold,
Stories of the heart unfold.
Whispers of the wind align,
Crafting tales of love divine.

Beneath the boughs of ancient trees,
We find solace in the breeze.
Every sigh, a hidden verse,
Echoes of the universe.

Chilled reverie, a dreamer's chase,
Finding beauty, finding grace.
In every heartbeat, in every sigh,
The magic of this life won't die.

The Night's Embrace

Softly falls the night's embrace,
Moonlit shadows, a gentle grace.
Stars awaken, twinkling bright,
Guiding dreamers through the night.

Whispers echo in the dark,
Hearts find solace, a tender spark.
Dreams take flight on silver wings,
In the stillness, the silence sings.

Night's caress, a calming balm,
Wrapping all in peace and calm.
Every gaze upon the sky,
Invites the soul to wander high.

A tapestry of starlit tales,
Woven through the cosmic gales.
In the night, we shed our fears,
Finding joy through all the years.

The moon whispers secrets old,
In its light, our dreams unfold.
In the night's sweet, soft embrace,
We discover our sacred space.

Dreamscapes of the Cosmos

In the quiet of the night,
Galaxies swirl like painted skies.
Whispers of stardust call my name,
Floating on cosmic lullabies.

Nebulas bloom in shades of blue,
While comets flash by with a grin.
Time unravels, space does too,
Lost in wonders, I begin.

Planets perform an ancient dance,
Under the watch of moonlit eyes.
Each twinkle holds a secret chance,
A wisp of fate in velvet highs.

Constellations speak of old,
Of tales that drift through endless space.
With every star, a story told,
In the warmth of their embrace.

Awake or dream, the lines are blurred,
In this realm where silence reigns.
Every heartbeat feels unheard,
In the magic of these cosmic chains.

Glistening Veil of Night

The world beneath a shimmering shroud,
Where shadows waltz in moonlit beams.
A tranquil hush, the stillness loud,
Wrapped tightly in silken dreams.

Stars like diamonds pierce the dark,
Painting stories on vast canvas skies.
Whispers echo, lighting a spark,
Of hope that never truly dies.

Cool winds drift through the open trees,
Carrying scents of distant shores.
Nature hums a gentle tease,
In the night when magic pours.

Beneath this veil, hearts find their way,
Guided by the glow of fate.
In the embrace of night's ballet,
Time slows down, we contemplate.

So let us dance beneath the stars,
And twirl in dreams both wild and free.
For in the cosmos, no one jars,
Our souls entwined in harmony.

Moonlight on a Shiver

The moon whispers secrets on the shore,
   Casting silver spells on the sea.
Waves shimmer softly, wanting more,
   In the embrace of night's decree.

A chill runs deep through the night air,
   As shadows stretch and sway around.
Nature hums her whispered prayer,
   In mysteries that know no sound.

Stars twinkle bright like eyes awake,
   Listening closely to tales untold.
In light's embrace, the world will shake,
   As dreams rise up from the cold.

The tranquil scene holds breathless weight,
While moths dance near the dimming light.
Each heartbeat matches night's soft gait,
   Lost in wonders of darkened flight.

So let us wander in this glow,
Where whispers weave through shades of night.
In moonlight's touch, we learn to grow,
   As shadows fade and dreams take flight.

A Dance of Stars

In the vastness of the night,
Stars ignite with flickering flame.
They twirl and sway, a wondrous sight,
Spinning tales none can tame.

The night sky holds a secret ball,
Where celestial beings twine.
Galaxies whisper, galaxies call,
In this dance, all hearts align.

Each constellation tells a tale,
Of heroes lost and dreams regained.
With every twinkle, hopes set sail,
In starlit skies, love is unchained.

Avalanches of light cascade,
On midnight's stage, as shadows play.
This cosmic dance will never fade,
As stars will shine till break of day.

So lift your eyes and join the song,
Let your soul sway with the night.
For in this dance, we all belong,
In the shimmering, endless light.

Glittering Chill of Forgotten Stars

In the night sky, whispers glow,
Flickers of dreams we used to know.
Each twinkle a memory, distant and bright,
Lost in the vastness of endless night.

Shadows dance where light once played,
Secrets held in the starlight's shade.
A chilly breeze carries tales afar,
Of glittering gleams from forgotten stars.

Time drifts slowly, like an old refrain,
Echoes of laughter caught in the rain.
We wander through realms, hearts intertwined,
Seeking the magic we left behind.

With every flicker, a story unfolds,
Of love and loss, of the brave and the bold.
The chill wraps around in a soft embrace,
In the arms of the cosmos, we find our place.

As dawn approaches with hues of gold,
The warmth of the sun breaks the night's cold hold.
Yet, in our hearts, the stars will remain,
A shimmering whisper of joy and pain.

The Frozen Horizon of Infinity

Glistening ice on the edge of sight,
Where earth meets heaven, a realm of light.
Horizons frozen in timeless grace,
Infinity stretches, a vast embrace.

Frigid winds breath life into the void,
Chilling breath of ages, none to avoid.
Every corner holds a promise untold,
In the depths of silence, a beauty bold.

Mountains shimmer with a blanket of white,
Veiling the secrets of day and night.
Boundless wonders in every direction,
A frozen charm, nature's perfection.

Stars gaze down with glimmering eyes,
Watching over as the world slowly sighs.
In stillness, the stories of ages unfold,
Of dreams that shimmer in the icy cold.

Yet deep in the heart, warmth starts to rise,
A flicker ignites, a phoenix that flies.
For even in freeze, there's life to ignite,
A dance of rebirth in the softest light.

Hushed Reveries in the Midnight Blue

In the quiet hour when the world sleeps,
Dreams weave softly, like whispers that creep.
Midnight blue drapes gently around,
Where secrets of the heart can be found.

Stars convene in a cosmic embrace,
Echoing thoughts that time can't erase.
Each moment a treasure, fragile and rare,
A tapestry woven with utmost care.

Silken shadows in the moon's tender glow,
Guide the soul where gentle winds blow.
Hushed reveries drift through the air,
In the stillness, we find solace there.

Time holds its breath, the world feels surreal,
Every heartbeat whispers a tender appeal.
In the midnight blue, our spirits take flight,
Swirling through realms of purest light.

When dawn breaks softly, passions will swell,
Yet the magic of night we'll cherish and dwell.
For in every hush, a story will brew,
In the depths of our hearts, the midnight blue.

Echoes of a Shimmering Silence

In the calm of dusk, shadows gently weave,
A tapestry of silence, hard to believe.
Each breath a whisper, each thought a song,
In the shimmering twilight where we belong.

The stars blink softly in tranquil embrace,
Holding the secrets of time and space.
Echoes of laughter dance on the breeze,
In the heart of the night, we find our ease.

Every flicker of light reveals the past,
Moments like diamonds, too precious to last.
In the stillness, our hearts start to blend,
Finding the harmony where souls transcend.

Like waves on the shore, memories rise,
Ripples of love under starlit skies.
A silence that sparkles, a sanctuary bright,
In the echoes of darkness, we find our light.

So let the night cradle us, gentle and clear,
In this shimmering silence, we'll hold each dear.
For in every pause, a universe gleams,
Echoes of calm in our wildest dreams.

Shivering Shadows Beneath the Cosmos

In the twilight's gentle grasp,
Whispers dance on midnight's breath.
Stars flicker in a tranquil mask,
Veiling secrets of life's depth.

Frozen echoes tell our tales,
Of dreams that flutter in the night.
Shadows weave through silver trails,
A symphony of soft twilight.

Beneath vast skies where silence sings,
The universe holds its breath tight.
In shadows cast by ancient wings,
We find solace in the light.

Across the cosmos, hopes take flight,
Beneath the shimmering, dark sea.
Each heartbeat pulses through the night,
In shadowed realms, we taste the free.

A tapestry of dark and bright,
We blend with stardust intertwined.
In shivering shadows, we ignite,
Awakening what lies behind.

Frigid Lullabies of Distant Galaxies

Cold winds carry whispered songs,
From stars that twinkle far away.
In silence, echoing among,
Galaxies where dreams gently sway.

Lullabies of frozen grace,
Drifting softly through the void.
In every heartbeat, we embrace,
The warmth that time has not destroyed.

Crystalline harmonies unfold,
Where shadows brush with moonlit beams.
In frigid grasp, the night is bold,
Cocooning us in quiet dreams.

Each note a bond, a timeless thread,
Connecting worlds and hearts alike.
In cosmic dance, where few have tread,
We find the spark, the fiery strike.

As galaxies wane and dawn awakes,
Frigid lullabies will remain.
A serenade that softly breaks,
Through shivering depths of our pain.

Glacial Radiance Above

Underneath the vast expanse,
Glacial light with a chilling kiss.
In stillness, we find our dance,
A moment wrapped in tranquil bliss.

Radiance glows in silver hues,
Reflecting gems in midnight's hand.
Each flicker a gentle muse,
Guiding dreams like grains of sand.

Amid the ice, our spirits soar,
Through endless realms where shadows glide.
In glacial glow, we seek for more,
Together, we embrace the tide.

Crystalline visions rise so clear,
Stars above, a precious guide.
In the cold, we shed our fear,
With glacial radiance, we abide.

Echoes of the universe call,
Inviting us to join the blend.
With each pulse, we feel the thrall,
In luminous dreams without end.

Flickering Lights in the Winter Veil

In the hush of winter's night,
Flickering lights from afar shine.
Each spark a whisper, soft and bright,
Wrapped in cold, the warmth is divine.

Beneath the snow, the world rests still,
A canvas white, serene, untamed.
With every flicker, hearts we fill,
The magic of the night proclaimed.

Stars peer down with knowing eyes,
Their secrets brushed by winds so light.
Through fragrant woods, a soft surprise,
Flickering lights, a wondrous sight.

Amongst the trees, a dance unfolds,
The winter veil, a shimmering thread.
In every glimmer, a story told,
Connecting paths we never dread.

As midnight shadows softly creep,
We find solace in the night.
Flickering lights, our dreams we keep,
In winter's embrace, pure delight.

Cosmic Frost

In the night, stars glimmer bright,
A blanket of frost, moon's soft light.
Galaxies dance in the silent air,
Whispers of dreams, the cosmos bare.

Frozen echoes, time stands still,
A shiver of wonder, a heart to fill.
Celestial jewels, silent parade,
In the cosmic frost, memories fade.

Softly they twinkle, tales to tell,
Of worlds unseen, where wishes dwell.
The universe breathes in a gentle sigh,
As frost laces stars, painting the sky.

Eternal embrace of ice and light,
Enfolding the heavens in tranquil night.
Cosmic visions in frosty air,
Infinite wonder, beyond compare.

Amidst the stillness, hearts align,
In cosmic frost, a love divine.
The universe whispers, soft and true,
A tapestry woven, me and you.

Celestial Sighs

In the vast expanse where stars unite,
Celestial sighs embrace the night.
Whispers of stardust drift and weave,
Carrying secrets of dreams we believe.

Softly they linger, time slows down,
In the hush of the cosmos, no frown.
Galaxies merge, a dance so grand,
Each sigh a promise, hand in hand.

Twinkling wonders, each shimmering gem,
A lullaby sung by the universe's hem.
Echoes of love in the quiet night,
Wrapped in celestial embrace, pure delight.

Beneath the moon's watchful gaze,
Hearts entwined in a timeless haze.
Celestial sighs breathe life anew,
As the cosmos whispers, I love you.

In the silence, desire ignites,
Two souls entwined on tranquil nights.
Celestial voices, soft and light,
Guide us gently through endless flight.

Twilight's Gentle Touch

Twilight whispers with a gentle sigh,
As shadows dance beneath the sky.
Colors blend in a soft embrace,
Nature's heart, a sacred space.

The sun dips low, painting gold,
Stories of wonder, quietly told.
Stars awaken, blinking bright,
In twilight's glow, banishing night.

Clouds drift slowly, a calming breeze,
Filling the air with tranquil ease.
Each moment cherished, a fleeting glance,
In twilight's arms, we find our dance.

The world slows down, just for us,
In the hush of dusk, no need to rush.
Tender moments wrapped in light,
Twilight's gentle touch feels so right.

Time stands still, a cherished hour,
Beneath the stars, we feel the power.
Nature whispers, our hearts in tune,
Under the watch of a silver moon.

Serenade of the Frost

In the quiet, frosty air,
Nature sings, devoid of care.
A serenade of winter's grace,
Whispers of magic in every space.

Snowflakes swirl like gentle dreams,
Dancing lightly in moonlit beams.
Each note a promise, soft and clear,
The frost's sweet song, we hold dear.

Frozen branches shimmer bright,
Adorned in whispers of the night.
Melodies linger, softly drawn,
In the serenade, we are reborn.

Every breath a frosty sigh,
In the stillness, time passes by.
Nature's lullaby, sweet and slow,
In the serenade, our spirits glow.

Wrapped in warmth, hearts intertwine,
In frosty serenades, love we find.
Together we stand, in winter's grace,
A cherished moment, our sacred place.

Celestial Silence

In night's embrace, stars gleam bright,
A tapestry woven, pure delight.
Whispers of cosmos drift and sigh,
Under the watchful, endless sky.

Planets dance, in their silent waltz,
Each heartbeat echoes, a cosmic pulse.
Galaxies whisper secrets old,
In the void, mysteries unfold.

The moon casts a glow, soft yet clear,
Guiding lost souls who wander near.
In celestial silence, hearts align,
Finding solace in the divine.

Nebulas swirl, colors collide,
Stories written, stars as our guide.
In the stillness, time drifts away,
Leaving behind the fray of the day.

Cosmic whispers, a lullaby sweet,
The universe's rhythm, slow and deep.
In this silence, we feel alive,
In celestial harmony, we thrive.

A Soft Glow Above

In twilight's grasp, a soft glow,
Illuminates the paths we go.
A gentle kiss from the setting sun,
Whispers of dreams, just begun.

Clouds painted pink, drift serene,
Nature's canvas, delicate and keen.
With each breath, the evening sighs,
As stars peek out from velvet skies.

Fireflies dance, in playful flight,
Their flickering light, a charming sight.
The hush of night, wrapped in bliss,
Promises held in the evening's kiss.

Moonbeams cascade, a silken thread,
In the quiet, where secrets are said.
Under this glow, hearts intertwine,
In shared silence, lives align.

A soft glow above, a guiding star,
Leading us home, no matter how far.
In the embrace of the night's soft hue,
We find our peace, and start anew.

Chilling Elysium

In a realm where whispers chill,
The air thickens with a spectral thrill.
Echoes linger from times long past,
In chilling Elysium, shadows cast.

A frigid breeze cuts through the air,
Like icy fingers brushing hair.
Moonlight breaks on crystal ground,
Beneath the stillness, old spirits abound.

Frozen lakes reflect the night,
Mirroring stars, a haunting sight.
The ethereal glow, so cold yet bright,
Guides lost souls through the endless night.

Branches creak, in a gentle moan,
Nature's sigh, a quiet tone.
Chilling winds weave tales untold,
In this Elysium, stories unfold.

Yet amidst the frost, warmth can grow,
Beneath the surface, emotions flow.
In chilling Elysium, we find our grace,
A delicate balance, a sacred space.

Ephemeral Starlight

In fleeting moments, stars ignite,
Ephemeral starlight, pure delight.
Cascading down, like whispered dreams,
Dancing through the night's soft seams.

With each twinkle, wishes take flight,
Hope rekindled in the dark night.
Patterns woven in silver and blue,
A canvas alive with wishes true.

Time slips away on celestial waves,
In starlit realms where the heart braves.
Each heartbeat echoes, a gentle call,
In this moment, we answer the thrall.

Guideposts shimmering, our path made clear,
In the embrace of starlight dear.
Transient beauty, a cosmic show,
Reminders of love in the night's glow.

Ephemeral whispers, fading fast,
Yet in our hearts, they're built to last.
In the dance of time, we find our light,
Embracing the magic of starlit night.

Nebulas in a Winter's Breath

In silence deep, the stars now gleam,
Nebulas swirl, a cosmic dream.
Cold winds whisper through the night,
Carrying tales of celestial light.

Frosted skies with a velvet hue,
Glimmers bright, a shimmering view.
Each breath taken brings forth delight,
As shadows dance in the moonlight.

Candles flicker in the crisp air,
Reflecting dreams woven with care.
In the stillness, our hearts align,
Beneath the vastness, divine design.

Stars like diamonds, scattered wide,
In winter's breath, they softly bide.
Timeless echoes of history's thread,
A cosmic tapestry, gently spread.

Silent moments, a tranquil embrace,
Lost in thoughts, in this sacred space.
As nebulas weave their subtle glow,
In winter's breath, we learn to flow.

The Icy Touch of Twilight

As daylight fades, the chill arrives,
The icy touch where shadows thrive.
Twilight drapes in hues of blue,
A whispered song, both soft and true.

Frosted branches, a glimmering lace,
Nature's art in a sudden embrace.
Each breath puffs like a ghostly sigh,
Under the vast, enchanted sky.

Stars awaken in a gentle dance,
In twilight's grip, the world holds its stance.
With fleeting moments, time stands still,
All hearts quiet, all souls fulfill.

Beneath the cloak of shimmering light,
Lies the magic of the approaching night.
The icy touch invites the dream,
To drift away on twilight's beam.

As darkness weaves a silken thread,
Painting landscapes where thoughts are fed.
In the calm of dusk, we find our way,
Through icy paths where shadows play.

Glimmering Hush of Celestial Bodies

In the quiet of night, they softly gleam,
Celestial bodies, a starlit dream.
Glittering hush on the velvet sea,
A cosmic canvas, wild and free.

Each twinkle tells a tale untold,
Whispers of space where wonders unfold.
Radiant pulses across the skies,
Glimmers bright as the daytime dies.

Galaxies spin in a waltz divine,
In the vastness where stars intertwine.
A serene hush fills the depths above,
Binding the cosmos with threads of love.

Reverie floats on a midnight breeze,
Caressing dreams with celestial ease.
In nature's dance, our spirits soar,
Through the glimmering hush, we explore.

As we gaze upon the galaxy's glow,
We find ourselves, lost in the flow.
A universe woven with infinite care,
In the hush of night, we breathe the air.

Night's Crystal Veil

Beneath the sky in shades of night,
Lies a crystal veil, shimmering bright.
Softly the echoes of silence call,
As mysteries linger, one and all.

Shadows stretch under silver beams,
Awakening thoughts, igniting dreams.
Each star a whisper, a secret held,
In night's embrace, all fears dispelled.

Reflections dance on the tranquil lake,
Mirroring wonders that night will make.
The crystal veil casts a soothing light,
Guiding our hearts through the deep of night.

In this stillness, we find our peace,
As the world spins in gentle release.
A lullaby sung by the moon so pale,
Wrapping us tight in night's crystal veil.

As dawn approaches, the veil will fade,
But in our souls, its beauty stayed.
Forever cherished, in memories kept,
In the tranquil night, our spirits leapt.

Whispers of the Midnight Sky

Stars twinkle softly, secrets unfold,
Time drifts slowly, stories untold.
Moonbeams dance lightly on silver streams,
Night wraps the world in echoing dreams.

Gentle winds carry a lover's sigh,
While shadows stretch beneath the sky.
Each whisper a promise, a fleeting breath,
In the stillness, we find life and death.

A symphony plays in the heart's embrace,
The night holds wonders, a sacred space.
Eyes gaze upward, where wishes take flight,
In the quiet, the stars shine bright.

Every heartbeat syncs with the cosmic tune,
Transience wrapped in the glow of the moon.
Echoes of laughter, a night so sweet,
In the darkness, two souls meet.

Whispers linger long after we part,
The midnight sky—a canvas for the heart.
Hope and magic twine, hand in hand,
Together we dream in this vast land.

Celestial Frost

Under moon's gaze, the world is still,
Nature sleeps softly, encased in chill.
Glittering frost blankets every tree,
A crystalline wonder, pure and free.

Stars shimmer bright in the cold night air,
Whispers of winter pull hearts to care.
Branches adorned with shimmering lace,
In the silver glow, we find our place.

Crackling silence, the world hushed tight,
Frost-kissed moments embrace the night.
Every breath mingles with icy dreams,
Woven together in starlit streams.

A dance of shadow and light does unfold,
Stories of warmth in the bitter cold.
With every heartbeat, our spirits soar,
In celestial frost, we seek for more.

Embers of love in the frost's gentle reach,
Lessons of solace that silence can teach.
In winter's cradle, we hold what's true,
Forever together, just me and you.

Luminous Fractals in the Night

Patterns emerge in the darkened skies,
Fractals of light where the mystery lies.
Every twinkle a puzzle, a tale untold,
In the vast tapestry, we search for gold.

Shimmering wonders weave stories bright,
Magic ignites in the heart of night.
Galaxies spiral, a cosmic thread,
Through the fabric of dreams, we gently tread.

In the silence, our thoughts take flight,
Drawing us closer in this celestial night.
Shapes intertwine like whispers of fate,
Dancing with shadows, we patiently wait.

Let the universe guide our souls to explore,
Each luminous fractal opens a door.
Through the cosmos, our journeys unfold,
In this intricate dance, we are bold.

Connected by starlight, we blaze in the dark,
Fireflies of hope leave their gentle mark.
Together we shine in the infinite sea,
In luminous fractals, forever we'll be.

Moonlit Solitude

In the moonlight's glow, a stillness found,
The world fades away, lost without sound.
Solitude wraps like a gentle shawl,
A serene embrace in the midnight hall.

Reflections shimmer on a silent lake,
Whispers of peace, heart never to break.
Thoughts take flight on this tranquil night,
In the soft glow, everything feels right.

Stars watch over like guardians near,
Cradled in silence, releasing all fear.
Breathing in calm, exhaling the past,
Moments of stillness, so precious, so vast.

The moon bears witness to dreams we weave,
In shadows of night, we learn to believe.
Every heartbeat echoes in time's sweet pause,
In moonlit solitude, we find our cause.

Embracing the quiet, we gather our thoughts,
In the realm of silence, battles are fought.
A journey within where our spirits can roam,
In solitude's arms, we always find home.

The Chill of Distant Worlds

In midnight's grasp, a whisper clear,
The icy breath of worlds so near.
Galaxies spin in silent grace,
With frozen dreams in endless space.

Stars glimmer faint, their secrets told,
Through cosmic realms, both brave and bold.
Together we wander, hand in hand,
In the chill of night, we understand.

Planets drift in a shroud of mist,
Moments lost in a starry tryst.
Each pulse of light, a tale begins,
Of distant realms where time never ends.

A nebula blooms, colors unwind,
In the vast expanse, new truths to find.
The chill caress of an unseen breeze,
Calls forth our dreams with gentle ease.

In this quiet dance, we hear the sound,
Of echoes lost, yet always found.
The chill of distant worlds invites,
Awakening our inner sights.

Echoes Beneath the Stars

Whispers of light in the velvet sky,
Carried by winds, the shadows fly.
Each flicker bright, each distant call,
Echoes beneath, where silence falls.

Time flows gently, a river's course,
Guiding the heart with cosmic force.
In the hush, we find our place,
Between each star, in endless space.

Voices of old in the twilight gleam,
Merging with hopes that softly dream.
Through galaxies vast, and nights so deep,
We gather the echoes, the secrets they keep.

A dance of shadows, a rhythm divine,
Across the heavens, we intertwine.
Moments unite, like flickers of light,
In the echoes beneath, we find our flight.

In the cosmic hum, we become one,
Our hearts align as we chase the sun.
Echoes of love, forever remain,
Beneath the stars, no joy, no pain.

A Cosmos of Crystal

In a realm where stardust flows,
Crystals form in radiant rows.
Light reflects in hues so rare,
A cosmos built with love and care.

Each facet sings of ancient lore,
Of worlds we dream and so much more.
Glistening dreams in the vast unknown,
A crystal song, we make our home.

Fragments dance in the endless night,
Woven softly in shades of light.
Like whispers floating on a breeze,
In this cosmos, our hearts find ease.

A tapestry spun from stars' embrace,
Crafts our stories, time cannot erase.
In every glimmer, a wish takes flight,
A cosmos of crystal, pure and bright.

Wonder abounds in this shimmering sea,
Reflecting the dreams we long to be.
In this realm of endless grace,
We find our truth, we find our place.

Frosty Luminary

A frosty glow on winter's night,
Illuminates the world in white.
Stars twinkle with a chilly gleam,
Whispering the dreams of a dreamer's dream.

Through icy breaths, a calm descends,
Where night and nature seamlessly blend.
The frosty luminary hangs so high,
Guiding our hearts as shadows sigh.

Snowflakes drift like whispers shared,
In the quiet beauty, we are bared.
Embracing the cold with spirits bold,
Under the luminary's watchful fold.

Amidst the frost, we dance in time,
To the rhythm of night's sweet chime.
Holding tight to the moments we claim,
Under the frosty star's bright name.

In silence profound, love's warmth ignites,
A frosty luminary blesses the nights.
As dreams take flight on the chill of air,
We find a light, beyond compare.

Whispers of the Night Sky

Stars twinkle softly above,
Carrying secrets from afar.
The moon whispers tales of love,
Guiding dreams like a shining star.

Winds carry the nighttime song,
As shadows dance beneath the light.
Echoes of twilight linger long,
In the embrace of velvet night.

Moths flit by on gentle wings,
Chasing glimmers with wild grace.
Each breath of night softly sings,
In this tranquil, sacred space.

Clouds drift like thoughts on the breeze,
Veiling mysteries in their flow.
Each moment a fleeting tease,
In the quiet that we all know.

Underneath the sprawling sky,
Hearts unite in silent prayer.
With every sigh the stars reply,
In the stillness, we find care.

Celestial Caress

The stars embrace the night so tight,
Whispers from the cosmic sea.
Moonlight bathes the world in light,
Kissing dreams as they long to be.

Galaxies swirl in a gentle dance,
Each twinkle a promise, soft and bright.
In their glow, the heart finds chance,
To wander through the endless night.

Comets trace their paths with grace,
Leaving trails of shimmering dust.
In their fleeting, vibrant race,
We find the solace we can trust.

The cosmos sings in colors bold,
A canvas painted with pure delight.
Every story in starlight told,
Wraps the world in their silver flight.

In the hush of a celestial breeze,
We breathe in the wonder, the vast unknown.
With every heartbeat, the universe sees,
That love's gentle touch is truly shown.

Frosted Dreams Above

In the chill of a starry night,
Frosted whispers coat the trees.
Dreams emerge in silver light,
Carried by the cold night breeze.

Icicles drip with glistening grace,
Mirroring the moon's soft glow.
Beneath the heavens, hearts embrace,
In the quiet, dreams softly flow.

Each snowflake dances in the air,
Filling the world with frosty gleam.
A serene calm beyond compare,
Wraps around the night's sweet dream.

In a hushed world, time stands still,
With whispers of hopes in simple tones.
The frosted ground beneath our will,
Cradles secrets in soft, gentle moans.

As the night deepens its embrace,
We find magic beneath the sky.
In every breath, a gentle trace,
Of dreams that stall, yet never die.

Luminous Nightfall

The sky ignites as daylight fades,
Colors blend in twilight's breath.
A luminous glow softens shades,
Painting shadows before their death.

Stars awaken from their slumber,
Twinkling bright like scattered jewels.
Night unfolds as we start to wonder,
A canvas where the universe rules.

Gentle breezes stir the leaves,
Whispering secrets of the night.
Each moment holds what it conceives,
In a world bathed in soft twilight.

In the hush, our dreams take flight,
Chasing echoes of the moon's delight.
Luminous glimmers draw us near,
In each heartbeat, magic is clear.

As night settles with quiet grace,
We find peace in the celestial show.
With every breath, we embrace this space,
Luminous tales in hearts now glow.

Ethereal Calm of the Cosmic Sea

Beneath the stars, a tranquil tide,
Waves of silence, where dreams abide.
Galaxies whisper in soft embrace,
Floating gently in cosmic space.

A canvas painted in shades so deep,
Where time stands still, as shadows creep.
Celestial breezes, a soothing balm,
In the vastness, we find our calm.

The moonlight dances on waves of night,
Reflecting wishes, dreams in flight.
A lullaby sung by twinkling eyes,
In the stillness, a soft reprise.

The endless ocean of the divine,
Each star a spark, a timeless sign.
In this realm, our hearts take wing,
To the cosmic sea, our spirits sing.

The Icy Glow of Ancient Light

Crystals shimmer under the moon,
Echoes of ages, a timeless tune.
Frost-kissed breath of the silent night,
Shimmers softly with ancient light.

In the depths of winter's gentle hold,
Stories of ice and fire unfold.
Stars draped in frost, a blanket wide,
Whisper of secrets that never hide.

Glimmers dance on the frozen lake,
A mirror of dreams, as heartbeats wake.
In the stillness, we become aware,
The chill of magic hangs in the air.

Through shadows cast by the starlit sky,
We wander 'neath the night's soft sigh.
With each flicker from far away,
Ancient tales come out to play.

Frozen Symphony of the Universe

Notes of silence linger in frost,
In the symphony, nothing is lost.
Each star a chord, in harmony,
Playing the tune of the galaxy.

The heavens hum with a tranquil grace,
Time's melody in a frozen space.
Gentle echoes of a cosmic choir,
Resonate softly, lifting us higher.

In this symphony, hearts align,
Woven together, a moment divine.
Celestial rhythms tune our fate,
In the chill, we resonate.

As constellations weave their art,
Music of starlight speaks to the heart.
Frozen beauty, a song so bright,
In the universe, we find our light.

Enchanted Silence of the Night Sky

In the hush of twilight's gentle breath,
Mysteries whisper of life and death.
The night sky wears a velvet veil,
Each star a story, a shimmering trail.

Silence wraps around the earth,
Cradling dreams, giving them birth.
Moonbeams sprinkle their silver dust,
Filling the darkness with hope and trust.

Winds of the night sing soft and low,
Guiding our thoughts where the shadows flow.
In this moment, all fears take flight,
Embraced by the magic of soft starlight.

As constellations dance in ballet,
Our souls find peace in the night's bouquet.
In this enchanted silence, we see,
The universe wrapped around you and me.

Nebulous Dreams in a Glacial Realm

In whispers soft where shadows dwell,
A realm of ice, enchanting, fell.
The dreams take flight, a spectral dance,
Beneath the stars, in cold expanse.

Glacial winds weave tales untold,
While moonlight drapes in silvery fold.
Each frozen breath a secret shared,
An echo of the dreams we dared.

The nightingale sings in frosted air,
Of fragile hopes and secrets rare.
With every beat, the heart can see,
The glistening path of destiny.

Through crystal spires, visions soar,
In nebulous realms forevermore.
The winter's heart beats wild and free,
In icy dreams, we find the key.

So let us wander, hand in hand,
Through this glacial, wonderland.
Where every star is softly spun,
And dreams in frost are gently done.

Fables of Frost and Stardust

Once upon a winter's night,
The stars awoke, a stunning sight.
With frost that glimmered in the dark,
They whispered tales of dreams' sweet spark.

A fable woven in the breeze,
Of frozen hearts that yearn to please.
Each snowflake falls, a story told,
Of love, of loss, of days of old.

From silver streams, the echoes rise,
Enchanting songs beneath the skies.
In every flake, a wish held tight,
A dance of dust in pale moonlight.

Embracing shadows, soft and bright,
The frost unfolds in pure delight.
A tapestry of love and light,
In winter's gaze, the world ignites.

So gather 'round the fire's glow,
For fables whispered in the snow.
In every heart, a tale remains,
Of frost and stardust, joys and pains.

Celestial Winterscape

In the stillness of the night,
The world aglow with purest light.
A celestial canvas, vast and wide,
Where dreams and stardust intertwine, collide.

Each snow-kissed branch a spark divine,
Reflecting glories of the time.
The heavens breathe, a tranquil song,
In winterscape, where souls belong.

The northern skies, a shimmering veil,
Where whispers of the cosmos sail.
With every star, a wish is caught,
In this cold realm, dreams are sought.

Frozen rivers, glistening bright,
Reflect the magic of the night.
A journey through the endless glow,
In celestial worlds, our spirits flow.

So wander forth in wonder's grace,
Through this enchanting, winter's space.
In every breath, a cosmic kiss,
In winterscape, we find our bliss.

Shadows of an Icy Horizon

In shadows cast by frost's embrace,
The horizon stretches, a silent space.
With every breath, the whispers cry,
Of glistening stars that fade and fly.

A tapestry of night unfolds,
With secrets wrapped in frigid folds.
Each icy breeze a tale of woe,
In shadows deep, where dreams may glow.

The landscape shifts, a ghostly play,
As shadows dance at break of day.
With every flicker, a promise fades,
In icy realms, the heart cascades.

Through twilight's grip, where echoes call,
In winter's grasp, we rise and fall.
A fleeting touch, a fleeting sigh,
In shadows deep, we learn to fly.

So walk with me, this chill divine,
Where icy horizons intertwine.
In frosty realms, our dreams take flight,
In shadows cast by long lost light.

Aurora's Embrace

Dancing lights in the sky,
Whispers of the dawn,
Softly they intertwine,
Awakening the morn.

Colors paint the night,
A canvas filled with dreams,
Embers of pure delight,
In nature's vivid beams.

Celestial embrace here,
As shadows start to fade,
Hope rises with cheer,
In hues that won't evade.

Radiant and alive,
The world begins to glow,
In beauty we arrive,
With every fleeting show.

Nature's hand bestows,
A masterpiece portrayed,
In every wave that flows,
Aurora's love displayed.

Cold Embrace of the Cosmos

Stars whisper in the dark,
Beneath a dome of night,
Infinite and stark,
They flicker with soft light.

Galaxies swirl and twine,
In the cold vast expanse,
Echoes of the divine,
In a celestial dance.

Wonders drift in the void,
Amongst the cosmic sea,
Silent, yet overjoyed,
In perfect symmetry.

A chill that grips the soul,
Yet warmth in every glow,
In the dark, we are whole,
Together as we flow.

Ever in this embrace,
We find our place to dream,
In the universe's grace,
A transcendent gleam.

Phantom Light

In shadows deep and wide,
A flicker calls my name,
It dances side by side,
A ghost of fleeting flame.

Soft whispers in the air,
Echoes of days gone by,
An essence lingers there,
Beneath the midnight sky.

Illusions lost in time,
Yet vibrant as the dawn,
In rhythm, they will chime,
As memories are drawn.

Phantom light within me burns,
A flicker of my past,
In the heart, it returns,
An imprint made to last.

Luminous and profound,
It guides through darkened night,
In silence, it's unbound,
This ever-present light.

Frosted Reverberation

Soft whispers in the snow,
With every step, a trace,
Nature's breath in a flow,
In winter's tender grace.

Crystal layers glisten,
Underneath the pale moon,
In silence, we all listen,
To this frosted tune.

A world wrapped in white,
Where dreams begin to freeze,
Each moment feels so right,
In the softest breeze.

Echoes of frozen streams,
Resound in chilly air,
A symphony of dreams,
In the world laid bare.

Awakening the heart,
To the wonders of night,
In beauty, we take part,
In this frosted light.

Celestial Frost

In the still of winter's breath,
Stars awaken, icy, bright,
Whispers float on frozen air,
Shimmering in the moonlight.

Branches draped in silver lace,
Nature's art, a crystal dance,
Every flake a fleeting grace,
Each glimmer holds a secret chance.

Fields of white stretch far and wide,
Footsteps crunch in quiet glee,
Underneath the starry tide,
Frozen realms of mystery.

The night wraps all in tender hush,
Timeless lullabies unfold,
In the frost, the shadows rush,
Stories from the night retold.

Dawn will come, with soft embrace,
Melting dreams of frosty flight,
Yet in the heart, a sweet trace,
Of the magic of the night.

Enchanted Night

Underneath the velvet sky,
Stars like jewels softly gleam,
Whispers carried on the sigh,
Magic flows in a dream.

Moonlight bathes the ancient trees,
Silver leaves in shadows play,
Nature dances with the breeze,
Casting worries far away.

Fireflies sprinkle gold around,
A symphony of gentle light,
In the dark, a tranquil sound,
Embracing peace, holding tight.

Crickets sing their serenade,
Notes of joy on stolen hours,
In this haven, fears allayed,
Nurtured by the night's soft powers.

Time suspended, moments blend,
In this realm where dreams take flight,
Under stars that never end,
We find our place within the night.

Infinite Chill

A breath of winter fills the air,
Crisp and sharp, it bites the skin,
Silence rests without a care,
Whispers hushed as night begins.

Blankets of snow, pure and white,
Covering the world in peace,
Stars illuminating the night,
Each in stillness finds release.

Frozen lakes reflect the sky,
Mirrors to the last light's glow,
In this calm, the heart can fly,
Seasons change, but winds still blow.

Flurries dance with every breath,
Nature weaves a colder tale,
In their flurry lives a depth,
Of a beauty that won't pale.

As the dawn prepares to break,
Chill subsides, the warmth will stir,
Moments pass, yet never ache,
For within chill, love will blur.

Ethereal Nightfall

As sun slips low, the shadows fall,
Colors blend in twilight hue,
Whispers dance around us all,
Embraced by night's gentle cue.

Stars ignite a canvas bright,
Scattered dreams across the sky,
In the quiet, soft delight,
With every twinkle, hopes can fly.

Dancing sighs of evening breeze,
Tales of old, stories spun,
Nature sings a song of ease,
As day dips low, and shadows run.

The world adorned in silver glow,
Every heart prepares to rest,
In night's charm, our spirits flow,
Grateful for this time, so blessed.

Moments pause, as starlight gleams,
Wrapped in peace, the night unfolds,
In the dark, we weave our dreams,
Ethereal heartbeats, soft and bold.

The Chill of Wandering Comets

Through the night they gracefully glide,
Trailing tails of stardust wide.
Each breath they take, the cosmos sings,
In the dark, a tale of wings.

Beneath the moon's watchful gaze,
In silent paths, they softly blaze.
Whispers of time in frozen air,
Echoing dreams with sparks to share.

Lonely journeys, secrets kept,
In the night where wonders wept.
Every glance a fleeting spark,
Guiding souls through realms so dark.

Chilling winds that guide their flight,
Flickering flames in the deep night.
With each passing, stories unfold,
Of distant worlds, of tales retold.

Wandering on, their paths align,
In cosmic dances, divine design.
While we stand, hearts beat in time,
With the chill of space, and rhythm's rhyme.

Twilight's Icy Gaze

In the dusk where shadows creep,
Twilight breathes, the world in sleep.
Stars peek through a frosty veil,
Silent stories in the pale.

An icy breath wraps the trees,
Whispers float like falling leaves.
Each twinkle, a glimmer of grace,
Reflecting light in a darkened space.

Cold winds dance, they sway and spin,
As twilight lets the night begin.
With every shadow softly cast,
A fleeting moment, forever passed.

In the chill, the heart beats slow,
As twilight casts its gentle glow.
With every blink, the stars ignite,
In frozen dreams of endless night.

A world wrapped in icy lace,
Twilight holds its secret place.
In the silence, winter's song,
Where it feels like we belong.

A Symphony of Stellar Whispers

In the vastness where silence reigns,
Stars hum softly, a chorus of chains.
Each note a flicker, light's embrace,
  In the night, we find our place.

Whispers of ancients, tales long spun,
The cosmos dances, the night begun.
Melodies flow on celestial streams,
In the depth of our stardust dreams.

Galaxies twirl in rhythm divine,
Harmonies of light, a cosmic line.
In the stillness, the heart expands,
As stardust echoes in our hands.

A symphony sung by astral souls,
Guiding us through shadowed shoals.
In the night sky, we listen still,
To the music of dreams, the universe's thrill.

As comets glide through the deep blue,
Their glimmers weave stories anew.
In this vastness, we find our song,
With silver threads where we belong.

Celestial Glow of the Arctic Night

In the Arctic, a glow so bright,
Dancing colors paint the night.
Auroras wave in vibrant streams,
Whispering secrets of icebound dreams.

Cold winds carry their soft tune,
Under the gaze of a watchful moon.
Nature's brush paints on the skies,
A spectacle where beauty lies.

Frozen landscapes hold their breath,
In this serenity, echoes of death.
Yet life sparkles in every flake,
As stars twinkle, the heavens awake.

The icy hush holds us in thrall,
In the warmth of night, we feel so small.
Yet within us, a fire ignites,
Reflecting the glow of celestial lights.

In every heartbeat, the universe sings,
Under Arctic skies, the magic clings.
A dance of lights, forever flows,
In the night, where true wonder grows.

Eclipsed by the Chill of Night

The moon casts shadows, cold and stark,
Whispers of silence fill the dark.
Stars blink gently, a watchful eye,
As time drifts quietly, passing by.

Frosty breezes weave through the trees,
A shiver dances with every breeze.
Night wraps the world in a soft embrace,
Hiding secrets in the dark space.

Flakes of white begin to fall,
Blanketing earth in a muffled thrall.
Breath becomes steam in the icy air,
Echoes of dreams float everywhere.

A distant owl hoots its song,
In the quiet night where shadows long.
The heart beats slow in this frozen light,
Eclipsed by the chill of the night.

Time stands still in the silver glow,
As nature sleeps, too soft to know.
Beneath the stars, the world feels right,
Embraced by the chill of the night.

A Tapestry of Frost and Twinkle

Gentle frost covers the ground,
Each flake a whisper, a soft sound.
Twinkling stars shine bright above,
Painting the night with endless love.

The trees wear coats of icy lace,
In this shimmering, magical place.
Crystals glisten in the moon's gleam,
Nature unfolds a frozen dream.

A chill bites softly at the nose,
As warmth of thought and memory flows.
Each breath taken, a cloud of white,
In this embrace of frosty night.

Night creatures stir beneath the frost,
In this beauty, nothing is lost.
A world transformed, a sight to see,
In the tapestry of night's decree.

Laughter echoes in the crisp air,
Moments captured, beyond compare.
In every heart, a brightened spark,
A tapestry woven deep in the dark.

The Veil of Celestial Dreams

Stars hang low like diamonds bright,
Blanketing all in soft, pure light.
A veil of dreams drapes the land,
Whispered wishes glide like sand.

The night sky sings a sweet refrain,
Wrapped in peace, far from pain.
Each twinkle tells a tale untold,
Carved in silence, precious gold.

Underneath this vast expanse,
Hearts awaken, ready to dance.
In the hush, we find our way,
Guided by dreams until the day.

With a gentle touch of starlit grace,
Hope glimmers in this timeless space.
The veil lifts softly, revealing bliss,
As we venture forth with every wish.

In cozy corners, shadows play,
Night invites us to drift and sway.
Celestial wonders breathe and gleam,
Wrapped in the veil of celestial dreams.

Night's Serenade in Ice

A symphony plays in the quiet night,
Notes of stillness, pure delight.
Ice crystals dance with every sound,
While the world spins softly round.

The moonlight strums on frozen trees,
Creating magic with every breeze.
Harmonies echo in the night air,
A serenade beyond compare.

Frosted flowers bloom in the dark,
Their beauty weaves a gentle spark.
In this chilly embrace we stand,
Listening closely, hand in hand.

Each whisper carries a secret wish,
As dreams are drawn from the night's dish.
Wrapped in warmth, we close our eyes,
Beneath the vast and starry skies.

Every moment drips like a song,
Where heartbeats rhythm, soft and strong.
Night's serenade in ice unfolds,
A timeless tale of dreams retold.

Mysterious Galaxy

In shadows deep, the stars align,
Whispers of worlds within the divine.
Galaxies dance, a cosmic waltz,
Secrets encased in celestial vaults.

Nebulas bloom with colors so rare,
Silent echoes pulse through the air.
Light years travel, stories untold,
In the embrace of the universe, bold.

Asteroids wander, a path unknown,
Stardust gathers, seeds widely sown.
Each twinkle holds a tale of its own,
In the vast night, dreams are grown.

Comets flash by, fleeting and bright,
Drawing our eyes, igniting the night.
Boundless beauty, a sight to behold,
In this mysterious galaxy, pure gold.

Eternal night with a radiant sheen,
The cosmos holds magic, still and serene.
Journey through time, through space, we roam,
In the heart of the galaxy, we find our home.

The Icy Tapestry

A quilt of frost on winter's breath,
Whispers of magic, a dance with death.
Crystal patterns in shimmering light,
Nature's artistry, a stunning sight.

Frozen rivers, still as can be,
Reflecting dreams, a silent decree.
Snowflakes twirl in delicate grace,
Each one unique, an ethereal trace.

In winter's grip, the world at pause,
Beauty crafted without a cause.
Nature's touch, a fleeting affair,
Wrapped in silence, a breath of air.

Icicles form, like daggers they gleam,
Guardians of secrets, frozen in dream.
A tapestry woven from cold, pure delight,
In the heart of the season, nothing feels right.

Under soft blankets of white, we confide,
Finding warmth where the cold cannot slide.
In the icy embrace, we find our way,
Through the tapestry's chill, we shall stay.

Shimmering Cold

A breath of frost in the morning light,
Fields adorned in a silvery white.
Whispers of winter dance on the breeze,
Nature's secrets, hidden in trees.

Glistening crystals on branches sway,
Each drop of dew holds the break of day.
Footprints crunch where the wild things roam,
In the shimmering cold, we find our home.

Moonlit nights with a shimmering glow,
Stars take flight, like the dreams we sow.
In the stillness, the world feels renewed,
Wrapped in warmth, our hearts are imbued.

Silent echoes in the crisp night air,
A magic lingers, beyond all compare.
In frost-kissed moments, our spirits unfold,
Lost in the beauty of shimmering cold.

As shadows stretch and the daylight wanes,
A soft embrace where quiet remains.
In each shimmering flake that dances free,
Winter whispers softly, just you and me.

Celestial Chill in the Air

Fog rolls in, a gentle caress,
Covering earth in a ghostly dress.
Stars twinkle down, a distant prayer,
In the stillness, a celestial affair.

Whispers float on the chilling breeze,
Nature's breath through the twisting trees.
Night unveils secrets, soft and rare,
Spirits of cosmos swirl in the air.

The moon hangs low, a sentinel bright,
Guiding lost dreams into the night.
Cool tendrils reach, wrapping us tight,
In the embrace of the divine light.

With every shiver, the world feels alive,
In the chill, our hopes revive.
Caught in the magic of the infinite fair,
We dance with the stars, breathing the air.

Celestial trails weave patterns so grand,
Mapping the dreams of the vast, distant land.
In every heartbeat, a universe shared,
In the chill of the night, we are never scared.

Aurora in the Silent Hour

In the quiet cloak of night,
Colors whisper, soft and bright.
Green and pink in swirling dance,
Nature's canvas, lost in trance.

Stars above, they nod and gleam,
Lighting up this waking dream.
A chill settles on the ground,
While the magic swirls around.

In stillness, beauty takes its stand,
With hues that paint the darkened land.
Each wave flows, a tender brush,
Where moments linger, hearts can hush.

Lost in wonder, souls unite,
Beneath the dreamy, pearly light.
The day is but a distant thought,
In this hour, peace is sought.

As colors wane, the night holds tight,
Embracing all in pure delight.
The dawn will break, yet for now,
Aurora speaks, and we allow.

Radiant Silence of Stellar Light

In the void where silence dwells,
Stars tell tales that time compels.
Whispers ride the cosmic breeze,
In this vastness, hearts find ease.

Galaxies twirl in dresses grand,
Holding secrets, hand in hand.
Each star a beacon, soft and clear,
With radiant silence, drawing near.

Nebulae glow in pastel shades,
Infinity in quiet parades.
A tapestry that shifts and sways,
Crafting moments in timeless ways.

Beneath the awe of endless night,
Eternity bathes us in its light.
Breathless starlight calls our name,
Boundless beauty, never tame.

In the vastness, we are small,
Yet united, we stand tall.
In radiant silence, we may find,
The universe is heart and mind.

A Dance of Luminescence and Frost

Moonlight spills on frozen ground,
In a world where dreams abound.
Frosty whispers kiss each tree,
A dance of light, wild and free.

Crystals shimmer, catching flare,
Every flake, a crafted rare.
In the night, the shadows play,
Where luminescence holds sway.

Glistening paths beneath our feet,
As nature's song becomes our beat.
Every twirl, a fleeting glance,
In this cold, we find our dance.

Hand in hand, we wander slow,
In a world wrapped up in snow.
The chill embraces, warm and bright,
A radiant waltz beneath the night.

As dawn approaches, colors bloom,
Breaking softly through the gloom.
The dance will fade, but in our hearts,
The memory of frost still sparks.

The Breath of the Cosmos in Winter

Frosted air, a soft caress,
Winter's hush, a quiet press.
Stars flicker in the frigid sky,
Breath of cosmos, whispers nigh.

Underneath a blanket white,
Dreams awaken, take to flight.
In the stillness, we can hear,
Echoes of the far and near.

Galactic wonders cast their glow,
Lighting paths we wish to know.
Each moment breathes with silent grace,
In this winter, time finds space.

Stardust glimmers on the frost,
In the night, no warmth is lost.
With every breath, the cosmos sighs,
A winter's tale beneath the skies.

As dawn breaks, the colors blend,
Winter's breath begins to mend.
In the heart of every soul,
The cosmos whispers, makes us whole.

Crystalline Dreams

In the silence of the night,
Stars twinkle like distant gems,
Whispering secrets to the moon,
While the world softly slumbers.

A shimmering veil of light,
Wraps the earth in gentle hues,
Painting visions in our minds,
Of a realm that's pure and bright.

Each breath carries a soft wish,
Floating on the cool night air,
Where hope dances with the stars,
In this canvas of pure bliss.

Mirrors of our lullabies,
Reflect the dreams we hold dear,
Crafting futures out of light,
In our hearts, love never dies.

With every spark a promise,
Of a day that's yet to come,
In the realm of crystalline dreams,
We chase the dawn, forever young.

Velvet Shadows

In the depth of twilight's grasp,
Shadows weave a silken tale,
As whispers brush against the skin,
Soft as twilight's breath unfolds.

The night wraps us in its folds,
Carrying secrets in the breeze,
While the stars take their places,
Guardians of our hidden hopes.

Each footstep on the cool ground,
Echoes stories left unsaid,
In the dance of soft night air,
Where emotions intertwine and blend.

A tapestry of dreams and fears,
Stitched with threads of deep desire,
In the velvet of the dark sky,
Our souls find a quiet place.

As we wander through the night,
In the shadows we find peace,
Embracing all that we have lost,
And the beauty within our sighs.

Cosmic Illumination

Beyond the haze of earthly light,
Cosmic wonders glimmer clear,
Galaxies swirl in silent grace,
Painting dreams in the cosmic night.

Every star a story told,
In the vastness of the void,
Twinkling hopes and dreams unite,
In a dance that never grows old.

Nebulae breathe, colors burst,
In this universe of wonder,
Awakening the spirit's spark,
As we journey, hearts immersed.

The moon bathes us in silver light,
Guiding lost souls on their way,
In a realm where time stands still,
Where night unfolds with sheer delight.

Underneath the cosmic dome,
We find ourselves, our place to shine,
In the brilliance of the night sky,
Cosmic illumination feels like home.

Cold Currents of Night

Beneath the stars, a chill descends,
Whispers of the night draw near,
As shadows creep across the land,
In the silence, dreams begin.

The moon hangs low, a silver eye,
Casting glimmers on the frost,
While the winds hum forgotten songs,
Of tales both lost and crossed.

In the darkness, echoes shiver,
With secrets buried deep and low,
The heart beats to the rhythm,
Of a world wrapped in cold flow.

These currents flow through every soul,
Connecting paths we cannot see,
Yet in the chill, warmth may arise,
From the bonds of history.

As the night breathes its icy breath,
We find solace in the stars,
Through cold currents we discover,
The warmth of who we really are.

The Frozen Gleam Above

Beneath the stars, a chill ascends,
Illuminating night, where silence mends.
The moon, a beacon in the frost,
Whispers secrets of the lost.

Icicles dangle from the eaves,
Crystals glisten, nature weaves.
Each breath a cloud, so soft and white,
In this stillness, pure delight.

Shadows dance on snowflakes spun,
A twinkling realm where dreams outrun.
Footsteps crunch on icy ground,
In this wonder, peace is found.

Frozen lakes reflect the sky,
Where distant echoes seem to fly.
A tapestry of cold and light,
Embracing winter, endless night.

In this realm, we find our way,
Guided by stars that softly sway.
Together wrapped in winter's seam,
We wander lost in frozen gleam.

Cosmic Embrace in Winter's Grasp

In winter's chill, the cosmos flows,
Stars align where cold wind blows.
Galaxies spin in a silent trance,
Under glimmering skies, we dance.

Frozen branches reach to space,
Cradling dreams in their embrace.
A nebula of ice and dust,
In this wonder, we place our trust.

Constellations mapped above,
Whisper tales of cosmic love.
The universe breathes, a gentle sigh,
In winter's hold, we learn to fly.

The frosty air, a breath divine,
Stars like diamonds brightly shine.
In this moment, still we stand,
Embraced by winter's gentle hand.

Beneath the vast, eternal night,
We find our paths in silver light.
In cosmic grasp, our hearts entwined,
In winter's love, our souls aligned.

Shimmering Echoes of Distant Worlds

Across the void, the echoes call,
Whispers from stars beyond the thrall.
Each twinkle brings a distant song,
In shimmering light, we all belong.

Time unfurls in a cosmic dance,
A ballet of light, a fleeting glance.
Waves of stardust wrap the night,
In darkened skies, there lies the light.

Planets twirl in their own way,
Chasing shadows through the play.
Galaxies swirl, in vibrant hues,
Paint the canvas we explore and choose.

The universe hums a gentle tune,
Reflecting dreams like the crescent moon.
Each heartbeat echoes in the dark,
A shimmering spark, our destined arc.

Through infinity, we too can roam,
Finding solace far from home.
In distant worlds, our spirits soar,
In cosmic echoes, forever more.

Frosted Dreams Beneath the Firmament

Beneath the stars, the snowflakes fall,
Frosted dreams beneath it all.
Blankets white on slumbering ground,
In tranquil beauty, peace is found.

The firmament whispers secrets old,
In icy breath, stories told.
Each flake a wish upon the night,
Carried softly in silver flight.

Luminous paths line the endless sky,
Where starlit wishes dare to fly.
Embers of hopes in the frost reside,
Beneath the firmament, dreams abide.

In quietude, beneath the veil,
Nature's pulse begins to sail.
With every shimmer, hopes renew,
In frosted realms, bright and true.

As dawn approaches, colors bloom,
Painting light upon the gloom.
In this dance of frost and light,
Our dreams emerge, taking flight.

Secrets of the Night Sky

The stars whisper tales of old,
In silken shadows, stories told.
Galaxies dance in the quiet space,
Infinite wonders in a cosmic embrace.

Moonlight bathes the world in glow,
Guiding dreams where soft winds blow.
Constellations form a mystic map,
Through velvet darkness, there's no gap.

A symphony of silence reigns,
Murmurs hidden in celestial chains.
The night sky holds secrets profound,
In its depths, lost hearts are found.

Each twinkling light, a wish unspoken,
A promise kept, a bond unbroken.
In the hush of night, hope ignites,
Whispers of dreams in starry nights.

So lie beneath this endless dome,
With each glance, you'll feel at home.
The secrets sway in the cosmic tide,
In the night's embrace, let love abide.

Frosted Whispers

Beneath the frost, the world sleeps tight,
Whispers of dreams in the pale moonlight.
Each breath of winter, a gentle grace,
As soft as shadows on a frozen face.

Crystal flakes fall like tender sighs,
Painting wonders across the skies.
Nature's hush in a silver hue,
A frosted tale that feels so true.

In the stillness, magic weaves,
With every glance, the heart believes.
Silent echoes of the night unfold,
In frosted whispers, stories told.

Branches adorned in glittering white,
The world transformed in the hush of night.
Every corner, a sparkling dream,
In the chilly air, whispers gleam.

Nature's canvas in frozen art,
Bringing warmth to the coldest heart.
With each snowflake, wonders arise,
Frosted whispers under the skies.

The Beauty of Frozen Dreams

In the heart of winter, dreams unfold,
Blankets of snow, a sight to behold.
Each flake a wish, unique and bright,
Whispers of magic in the soft moonlight.

Frozen landscapes, a world so still,
Embers of hope in the cold wind's chill.
Every moment wrapped in serene grace,
A symphony of silence in this frozen place.

Mirrored lakes like shards of glass,
Reflecting dreams as moments pass.
In every corner, beauty gleams,
The world awash in frozen dreams.

Frosted trees with branches wide,
Harbor secrets that they confide.
Nature's palette of white and blue,
In stillness, the heart finds something new.

So cherish the chill and icy embrace,
In frozen dreams, we find our place.
With every glance, let your spirit soar,
In the beauty of winter, forevermore.

Stars Through Frosted Glass

Through frosted panes, the stars ignite,
Casting dreams in the still of night.
Each sparkle dances, a fleeting kiss,
Whispers of wonder in a world like this.

The chill wraps round like a tender hug,
In the midnight air, the heart grows snug.
Under the frost, secrets lie,
Stars above in a velvet sky.

Each twinkle tells of journeys far,
In the depths of night, a guiding star.
Through the glass, they shine so bright,
Illuminating paths in the darkest night.

A cosmos full of ancient lore,
Seductive tales from the heavens soar.
Through the frost, we glimpse the vast,
Echoes of futures and shadows of the past.

As night surrenders to dawn's warm glow,
The stars whisper tales that gently flow.
In the frost, dreams drift and dance,
Through frosted glass, we find romance.

Echoes of the Cosmos

Stars whisper secrets, distant and bright,
Galaxies dance in the velvet night.
Each twinkle a story, ancient and wise,
Echoes of time beneath endless skies.

Nebulae glow with colors surreal,
Painting the heavens, a canvas to feel.
Dreams of explorers in silence take flight,
Boundless the wonders that shimmer in light.

Glimmering Frost

Morning unveils a glimmering scene,
Frost coats the world in a shimmering sheen.
Each blade of grass wears a crystal crown,
Nature's soft whispers, a delicate gown.

Sunlight awakens, a golden embrace,
Chasing the chill, quickening pace.
Patterns like lace on each windowpane,
A fleeting beauty, both silent and plain.

Nocturnal Serenade

Moonlight spills softly over the land,
Night creatures stir to a tune unplanned.
Crickets play songs in the cool evening air,
Mysteries mingle with whispers to share.

Stars twinkle, casting a magical glow,
Shadows waltz slowly, as breezes blow.
In the hush of the night, dreams start to soar,
Wrapped in the calm, we long to explore.

Ice-Kissed Twilight

Twilight descends in a frosty embrace,
The day softly sighs, finding its place.
Icicles shimmer like diamonds in line,
As daylight surrenders, the stars start to shine.

The trees stand silent, all draped in white,
Bathed in the glow of the coming night.
Whispers of winter drift through the pines,
A serene lullaby that gently aligns.